101 FACTS

Every Person Should Know About God

Chuck Coggins

101 Facts
Every Person Should Know About God
ISBN 978-1-936314-39-3
Copyright © 2011 Chuck Coggins

Chuck Coggins
P.O. Box 2481
Broken Arrow, Ok 74013

Published by
Word & Spirit Books
P.O. Box 701403
Tulsa, Ok 74170
www.wordandspiritbooks.com

Book Endorsement

One of the disciplines of Bible study I discovered years ago is that every time I open the pages of the scripture and read its God-breathed contents, I search to discover more about the nature and character of God. I encourage you to develop the same discipline each time you read the Bible—observe what is revealed about God, God's character, God's heart and mind, God's activity, and God's reign in all of creation. Look for God's will and how God desires to be at work in your life and through your life.

In this short, yet powerful book, Chuck Coggins delivers 101 brief readings which celebrate the marvelous God we proclaim, worship, and serve. Rather than rush through the readings, I hope that you will savor each reading, taking the opportunity to meditate on its contents. Doing so will bring you into new discoveries of our amazing God, into celebration of God's character and work, and God's promises of His faithfulness in your life.

In awe of God,

Dick Read
Pastor of Discipleship
Asbury United Methodist Church
Tulsa, Oklahoma, USA
www.asburytulsa.org

Foreword

When Chuck began compiling these Bible studies into a book, we didn't know the impact that it would have on our own life. This unique book seemed to have a life of its own. As God's Word often does, it not only *is* life but it *gives* life to those who will open their heart and minds to it. One of our first experiences sharing the book was in a church in Kenya. Chuck asked ten members of the audience to pick a number between 1 and 101.

As the people called them out in random order he wrote them down on a piece paper. Starting with the first number he turned to that page in the book and he began to speak. Then he turned to the next number and the next. It was amazing how each thought flowed together seamlessly from page to page in perfect harmony. It was communion Sunday for their church and it so happened that the last page number that was called out was a scripture and commentary on communion! That led us so perfectly right into the breaking of His Bread and drinking of His Cup. Communion had a special presence that morning and Chuck could not have done better if he had taken time to plan out his sermon.

We have used this modest book for daily devotions. We have looked to it for encouragement for ourselves and to share with others. We have asked friends to pick a number from the book only to watch their faces brighten as they realize it is speaking directly to something they have been facing or going through and on that page they found peace, joy, faith, or comfort.

This book is in no way a comprehensive book of facts, but has been kept simple in order to provoke thought and meditation in the scriptures. The concept of the book is to stimulate your thinking for more in-depth studies on your own or in a group setting. As we know Romans 11:33 says, "O the depth of the riches both of the wisdom and knowledge of God! How unsearchable are his judgments, and his ways past finding out!" Our hope is that as you read this book you will *find out* a little more about God, His Son Jesus, and the Holy Spirit as you open the pages and enter into *101 Facts Every Person Should Know About God*. Pick a number!

Connie Coggins

1

God so loved the world that he gave his only begotten son, so that whoever believes in him would not perish, but have eternal life.

JOHN 3:16

God's deep and devoted love for us was fully demonstrated when Jesus carried the cross all the way to Calvary. He willingly gave up His life and paid the severe penalty that we could not pay—and removed our sins that had separated us from God. Jesus is the open doorway into the Kingdom of Heaven where every person can enter freely and enjoy a new life made right with God.

2

God is able to save completely, perfectly, finally, for all time and eternity those who come to Him through Jesus Christ.

HEBREWS 7:25

When some people think of being saved or receiving salvation they mistakenly picture only their sins forgiven and a chance to go Heaven when they die, but salvation is much more than that. Everyone should understand when we come to God through Jesus Christ, He saves us completely. Salvation includes peace of mind, strength, health, provision, and total well-being. God's grace, favor, and blessings of every kind are yours in Christ.

3

God is love and he that dwells in love dwells in God and God in him.

1 JOHN 4:16

God doesn't just have love—He is love. His every thought and action toward us is love. His plans for us are only good and He wants us to have everything we need. He watches over us carefully and with tenderness—He even shares our sorrows. He wants the best for us so He sent the Shepherd to bring us back from our wanderings. He really does love you and me.

4

God inspired all scripture and it is useful to teach us what is true and to make us realize what is wrong in our lives.

2 TIMOTHY 3:16

The Bible is not a book that man made up. However, God inspired man and allowed man to participate in the writing of it. Every word in the Bible is from God and it is good and true. It is useful to teach us what is profitable and to make us realize what is detrimental to our lives. It corrects us when we are wrong and teaches us what is right.

5

God will prepare you for what He's called you to be and He will fill your good ideas with His own energy so they will amount to something.

2 THESSALONIANS 1:11

One wise teacher once stated, "When preparation and opportunity collide—then comes success." I agree with that statement because I know that God is always preparing and equipping us, giving us His thoughts and good ideas, then energizing us to achieve them. He also strengthens us with His greatness so that we can become the people we were meant to be—accomplishing His will and fulfilling His purpose for our lives.

6

God chose us in Christ before he made the world to be holy and without fault in his eyes.

EPHESIANS 1:4

You are no accident. God didn't pick you out because He had to or was forced to. He was not even obligated to. But because of His great love, God planned you and chose you—even before time began. But the good news doesn't just stop there! Now, because of the blood of Jesus, God sees no more faults in you and considers you holy, blameless, and unspotted in His sight.

7

God through Jesus Christ will judge people's secret thoughts.

ROMANS 2:16

We have no secrets before God—He knows and sees all that we do. Everything that is hidden will eventually be brought into the open, and every secret will be brought to light. The day is coming when God will judge us through Jesus Christ and we will be required to give an account of everything we've ever done—all our thoughts and actions—even the ones we *thought* were secret.

8

God has showered his kindness on us, along with all wisdom and understanding.

EPHESIANS 1:8

If you stand out in a shower you're going to get wet. If you stay there long enough you'll get drenched. God poured out His kindness to us through Jesus and along with that He has given us the chance to live intelligently in this world by sharing His wisdom and understanding with us. We should stand out in the shower of God's kindness and wisdom every day—and become saturated.

9

―――∞∞∞―――

God will bless us and all the ends of the earth shall fear Him.

PSALM 67:7

God wants to bless you. You must believe that. He wants His full blessings to flow directly to you. Yes, He made it all available through Jesus Christ. That's why we bow our knee to Him, because He is Lord of everything—even the blessings. Eventually, everyone will bow and all the ends of the earth will fear Him and give Him the honor and respect due to His Holy Name.

10

*God is a faithful God keeping His covenant
of love to a thousand generations of those
who love Him and keep His commands.*

Deuteronomy 7:9

God is a faithful God who has pledged to keep a covenant of love enduring for a thousand generations to those who love Him and keep His commands. We can be confident this covenant is real—because God has sealed it by the blood of His Son Jesus. If you're among those who love Him and keep His Word—then nothing can ever break this promise He has made with you.

11

God is light, and in Him is no darkness at all.

1 JOHN 1:5

Sometimes you go away from a conversation with someone and you don't know where you stand—and you can't really understand what just transpired. That won't happen with God. He doesn't hide His true intentions and will never leave you in the dark or be dishonest with you. With God in our life the lights come on, wisdom prevails, problems are solved, answers come, and everything takes on meaning and definition.

12

———〰〰〰———

God's word will not return empty but accomplishes what He desires and achieves the purpose for which He sent it.

ISAIAH 55:11

God doesn't speak just to listen to Himself talk. God's words always have a meaning to them. They are always directed to some purpose, sent to accomplish some task. God's words are not idle, lifeless, or useless—but His words perform what He pleases and achieve the job He sends them to do. We should be like God and mean what we say and carry out the things that we've spoken.

13

God is good and His love endures forever; and His faithfulness continues through all generations.

PSALM 100:5

Jesus said there is only one who is good, and that is God. He was so right. Human love grows cold, people stumble and quit, but God's love never fails—it endures forever. He is faithful even when we're not. He's good and will remain good, even though we don't deserve it. God will continue to show His unfailing love to every generation through Jesus Christ—now that's good news.

14

God created man in His own image, in the image of God He created him; male and female He created them.

GENESIS 1:27

Men and women are the only creative creatures on earth. Not one member of the animal kingdom has ever created a tool or developed a device capable of assisting others in life. People are creators like God, made in His very image and likeness. Those who are born again are heirs of His Kingdom. If you are born again then let His nature rule and bring divine order to your life.

15

God, in the beginning, prepared, formed, fashioned, and created the heavens and the earth.

GENESIS 1:1

The earth is not the result of some accidental, haphazard cosmic blast, nor the result of a huge chaotic celestial boom without the foreknowledge of an infinitely wise creator. When you look for a moment at the delicate balance of this world's ecosystem, you cannot deny His intelligent design. God—the original inventor—prepared, formed, fashioned, and created the heavens and the earth for His glory and for our wonder.

16

God has created all things for His pleasure, and He alone is worthy to receive all glory and honor and power.

REVELATION 4:11

God created the earth and all the creatures in it for His own enjoyment. Even mankind was made to bring pleasure and honor to Him. The scriptures tell us that it satisfies God when we keep His commandments and do those things that are good in His sight. Keeping God's instructions is really not an option if we want our lives to reflect His glory and bring honor to His name.

17

God predestined us to be adopted as His sons through Jesus Christ.

EPHESIANS 1:5

Adoption establishes guardianship and is legal and binding. Before all time, God chose us to be His own children and has taken on the responsibility as our complete caregiver and not just until we're eighteen years of age—but forever. He paid all the fees and satisfied all legalities of this transaction by the blood of His Son. So now we are recognized as members of God's family through Jesus Christ.

18

*God sealed us with the Holy Spirit who is
the deposit guaranteeing our inheritance.*

EPHESIANS 1:13

When an earthly king seals an important
document, he places a drop of hot wax onto the
seam. Then he thrusts his ring, which is
embossed with the emblem of his kingdom, into
the hot wax, leaving his official insignia. In this
same way God has sealed us with His official
Kingdom seal—His Holy Spirit. We have been
specially marked as royalty and guaranteed a
portion of the King's treasures.

19

God is able to make all grace abound to you.

2 CORINTHIANS 9:8

An acrostic is a form of writing in which the first letter of each line spells out a word or a message. An acrostic for grace looks like this:

G od's

R iches

A t

C hrist's

E xpense

It cost Jesus everything to provide us with His grace. God is not holding anything back, but now at Christ's expense He is able to make all grace abound to us.

20

God will rescue His people just as a shepherd rescues his sheep and they will sparkle in His land like jewels in a crown.

ZECHARIAH 9:16

If we go astray—or it might be more accurate to say, *when* we go astray, because we all do—God, being the Good Shepherd that He is, will come and rescue us. Sheep need to follow the Good Shepherd closely because they are easily distracted and wander off. We should always stay close to the Lord—so our lives will sparkle like radiant jewels in His royal crown.

21

God wants us resting in the hope of eternal life that He promised to us before the world or time began.

TITUS 1:2

There is a rest for the people of God. He has designed their journey with special places of refreshing all along the way. The self-motivated person who tries to find satisfaction, lasting pleasure, or peace of mind without submission to God will wrestle endlessly, become weary, and lose their sense of purpose. But the child of God enjoys the peace that passes understanding— because they trust in the everlasting God.

22

If you will believe in your heart and confess with your mouth Jesus is Lord, you will be saved.

ROMANS 10:9

I think it's easy to recognize that everything in life works on this principle of believing and speaking. What we believe in our hearts we speak about. What we speak about we act on. If you will believe in your heart that Jesus is who He says He is and speak that with your mouth— you can be transformed into the happy successful person God always intended for you to be.

23

―⊗⊗⊗―

God has freely given us His glorious grace through Christ.

EPHESIANS 1:6

There is no payment you could make, no work you could perform, no fortune you could exchange, and no promotion you could attain that would enable you, or qualify you to receive God's grace. But God has chosen to give it to you freely anyway because of what Christ has done. And they that receive an abundance of grace and the gift of righteousness shall reign in life through Jesus Christ.

24

God has made His mystery known to His saints, Christ in us the hope of glory.

COLOSSIANS 1:26

Unless we're born again we can't see the world God sees and we surely cannot enter the glorious world where God lives. How could we even think for one minute that we might be able to unravel the mystery of "Christ in us the hope of glory"? It is not possible to understand that unless we are born again—then God begins to reveal all of His Kingdom mysteries to us.

25

God is able to do whatever He promises.

ROMANS 4:21

All of God's promises are yes and amen. God delivers on His word to us. He will not speak and change His mind. He is not like us who fail and forget and sometimes, even lie. God is a God of His word and His promises are true and not subject to change. God is able. It is impossible for God to lie. We can count on Him—God will always deliver.

26

❦

God spared not His own Son but delivered Him up for us all and with Him has freely given us all things.

Romans 8:32

This reminds me that for our eternal good, God has already made the ultimate sacrifice in the death of His Son Jesus. So I have to ask myself, "Could God somehow forget to provide for us, neglect to help us, or withhold good from us now in this life?" The answer is, "Absolutely not, of course not." But along with the sacrifice of Christ, He has freely given us all things.

27

God's glory is declared by the heavens and the skies proclaim the work of His hands.

PSALM 19:1

Why does the sun hold its firm place in the sky and provide light and warmth to our planet? Why does the moon lighten the night and assist the sea's tide? Why do the stars glimmer with white light against the black curtain of the cosmos? I think that answer is easily understood—to proclaim His glory, to declare His majesty, and to show forth the work of His mighty hand.

28

God is faithful and He will not let you be tempted beyond what you can bear.

1 CORINTHIANS 10:13

With every temptation He has made the way of escape providing a doorway out. Jesus is the door. He won't abandon you or take you half way—but He'll go all the way with you—not leaving you to deal with temptation on your own. Remember, Jesus was tempted in all points as we are, yet without sin. Ask God for help when facing temptations and sin. Jesus overcame the world.

29

God is for us and God is on our side. So who can succeed if they try to come against us?

ROMANS 8:31

Some have been told that God is mad at them. They have been unsure whether God likes them or not. They wonder if God favors some more than others. I want you to know that God likes you, He is for you, He's on your side, He is pulling for your success and He openly opposes those who would try to hinder you. So be encouraged—God is on your side.

30

God has given to every man the measure of faith.

ROMANS 12:3

Everybody gets to start at the same point where faith is concerned. God does not favor anyone above another but has generously given to each person the same measure of faith. This measure is a portion of Gods faith—it's the same faith He used to frame the universe and raise Christ from the dead. The same life-giving, world-creating faith is inside each of us—we should use it.

31

God is not unjust and will not forget your work and the love you have shown Him as you have helped and continue to help His people.

HEBREWS 6:10

God keeps good, precise, and accurate records. He is a great accountant. He knows your work and will not overlook the love you have shown in His name. He will never forget to pay or compensate His workers. Jesus said when you help God's people you are helping Him and you will receive your reward. If you remain faithful, working for Him, when your payday comes you will not be disappointed.

32

God will make you successful in everything, giving you many children, abundant livestock, and fields that produce bountiful harvests.

DEUTERONOMY 30:9

God will make you successful if you think about His Word day and night and carefully do all He tells you to do—then you will find your way in this world and you'll profit in everything you do. God will make you fruitful in your field and cause you to have an abundant harvest in every area of your life. He promised that whatever you put hand to will prosper.

33

God examines your heart and knows everything about you.

PSALM 139:1

God looks intently on the heart of man. He examines everything about it closely and judges everything within it according to His Word. He created you and me and is watching over us. He knows everything about us. That's good because many times we do not understand ourselves or know why we respond to situations as we do. When that happens we should ask God for help comprehending our own hearts.

34

God forgives our sins, heals our diseases, redeems us from death and destruction, crowns us with loving kindness and tender mercies fills our lives with good things and renews our youth like the eagles.

PSALM 103:3

Forgiveness, healing, deliverance, kindness, mercy, good things—even our youth renewed like the eagles. What a set of promises and all in one scripture! If we never had any more promises concerning the benefits of salvation—this could be enough to sustain us. And just think, these are only some of the benefits of serving God. If we will take hold of these words—our lives will never be the same!

35

God promised to meet all your needs according to His riches in glory by Christ Jesus.

PHILIPPIANS 4:19

This promise is not just for anyone—God promised it to givers. Reading this verse in context, we see the Apostle Paul was commending the saints who had contributed to his needs on the mission field. God gives His goodness to everyone—but He meets all the needs of givers. When you are always participating in meeting the needs of others, then you can truly claim this promise as your own.

36

God promised that we could do all things through Christ who strengthens us.

PHILIPPIANS 4:13

That is a wide open promise from God, taking the limits off of everything. Life presents us with many challenges—some are beyond our strength or natural abilities to overcome. We will even face serious situations that require God's special intervention. In those times we can boldly say in the face of impossibilities, "I can do all things in the name of the Lord Jesus Christ who gives me His strength!"

37

God promised to give us direction and make our path straight if we recognize and acknowledge Him in everything.

PROVERBS 3:6

If you want to go around and around in circles then try relying only on your own navigational skills. When you finally tire out let God have the helm. God is not your First Mate—He is the Captain of your ship. He is the one who has charted out the course for your life and He knows exactly where you're going and how to get you there safely and on time.

38

God is generous and will give wisdom to anyone who asks for it.

JAMES 1:5

God loves it when we don't have the solution to our problems. He delights in it when we come to Him to find the answers to life's questions and concerns. When we ask He gives counsel liberally and without hesitation the wisdom we require and does not make us feel ashamed for asking. His only condition is that we ask in faith and believe that we receive it—and it's ours.

39

God is able to do exceeding, abundantly above all we ask or think according to the power that works within us.

EPHESIANS 3:20

The definition of exceeding is: *to do extremely more than is expected* and the meaning of abundantly is: *a profuse and plentiful supply*. God can easily exceed all of our expectations and He is able to supply much more than we ask, but we have a part to play. This power is released *according to* and in *direct proportion to* the power of His Word that is actively working in us.

40

God promised to give us eternal life through Jesus Christ.

JOHN 3:16

Eternal life doesn't begin when we get to heaven—it starts when we're born again. We can and should experience living in eternal life through Jesus Christ every day. When we die, then it will be time to explore the glory and vastness of heaven alongside our friends and loved ones who have preceded us in Christ. It's comforting to know that He has prepared a place for us in eternity.

41

God is faithful, by whom ye were called unto the fellowship of His Son Jesus Christ our Lord.

1 CORINTHIANS 1:9

God is not sporadic, inconsistent, fickle, nor impulsive. Just the opposite, He is stable, unwavering, loyal and trustworthy. God is faithful and has called us into fellowship with His Son Jesus Christ—He has opened up a way for true fellowship with us. He wants to grow in friendship with us and desires we experience communion with Him every day. God is interested in developing a long-term relationship with you.

42

God is able to establish you.

ROMANS 16:25

Every builder knows that a house is only as good as the foundation it's built upon. If the foundation crumbles under the weight of the structure the entire house will come down. God is able to establish us on a foundation that is sure, tried, and proven—Jesus Christ, *"Our Rock of Ages."* If we build our house on that *"Rock,"* then our lives will not be destroyed by our problems.

43

God sent His only begotten Son into the world, that we might live through Him.

1 JOHN 4:9

God sent Jesus, His only begotten and uniquely born Son, into the world. He was the Word that became flesh and lived among us. And now through His Word we begin to experience fullness and abundant life every day. When we choose to follow Him and do what His Word reveals, we are living out His life. Then His blessings flow to us and through us to the world around us.

44

God is greater than our heart, and knows all things.

1 JOHN 3:20

God is greater than all things—including our own hearts. Much of the time we don't even know what's in our own hearts, but He does. The Father, who knows all, even knows what the Holy Spirit is praying when He pleads for believers in harmony with God's will. It is then that everything begins working together for good to those who love God and are called according to His purpose.

45

---⚬⚬⚬---

God wants us to live in peace, help the weak, and be patient with everyone.

1 THESSALONIANS 5:14

God said if we would make our prayers and requests known unto Him that we would enjoy peace that passes all understanding. And He also promised that He would keep our hearts and minds through Christ our Lord. When we are at peace we are more patient and able to help others. Then we can reach out to the weak with greater strength and power that comes from God within us.

46

God is able to build you up and give you an inheritance with all those He has set apart for Himself.

ACTS 20:32

God is a wise master-builder. He is building you from the ground up. You're under construction. He is working on your project every day. He is keeping you strong, edified, and growing into the fullness of His stature. He's working His plan in you and He will complete you in Christ. He has also set you a part for Himself and has prepared a special inheritance for you—reserved in heaven.

47

God is able to deal gently with your ignorance.

HEBREWS 5:2

Have you ever been scolded by someone when you gave a wrong answer? Or embarrassed by your poor test scores because you failed to study and do your homework? Here's some good news, the Lord will not mock or ridicule you about your lack of knowledge. But He tenderly and purposefully instructs His children leading them into the knowledge of the truth. We can all grow in that kind of environment.

48

God is able to shut the mouths of lions.

DANIEL 6:20

God supernaturally protects His people. Daniel found out about the faithfulness and power of God to protect him in a lion's den. God sent His angels to shut the mouths of those hungry lions and Daniel was not harmed. Maybe you have found yourself in a situation needing God's strong care and deliverance. You can trust Him—God is able and He will shut the mouths of lions for you too.

49

God is able to deliver you from the blazing furnace.

DANIEL 3:17

How hot can a furnace of circumstances get? Very hot! The three Hebrew leaders of the King's province, Shadrach, Meshach and Abednego, found out as the wrath of the King was enflamed against them. But then suddenly God showed up in the fire, set them free, and devoured their adversaries. We can trust God in the worst of situations and see His saving power—even in a blazing furnace of fire.

50

God is able to guard what you entrust to Him.

2 Timothy 1:12

Sometimes thieves slip past even the most sophisticated alarm systems, break down security codes and disarm man's strongest defenses. We must not rely on them but on God, He cannot fail. He is fully armed and supernaturally equipped, able to protect that which we entrust to Him. When we give Him our life, finances, health, family, and our future we can trust that in His care we are completely and entirely secure.

51

God is able to keep you from falling.

JUDE 1:24

My Dad had a favorite saying that went like this, "Son, experience is what you get when you are expecting something else!" That's what Peter found out as he decided to walk on the water with Jesus. When the strong winds and violent waves came against him, he cried out saying, "Lord, save me!" Immediately Jesus stretched forth His hand and caught him. You may fall— just don't forget to call!

52

God is able to help you when you are being tempted.

HEBREWS 2:18

Every person is faced with a full array of temptations to sin. We should not try to cover up or simply dismiss a thought that would try to lead us astray, but acknowledge it to God and ask Him for help to overcome the temptation. God is not taken off guard by the confession of our weaknesses, but is ready to strengthen us and give us the power to resist sin.

53

God has brought you into His own presence by the blood of Christ.

COLOSSIANS 1:22

If Christ had not entered in to the Holy of Holies sprinkling His own blood on the mercy seat of God, we'd have no access into God's Holy presence. But because He shed His blood for our sins, washing us, cleansing us, and putting on us His robe of righteousness, we are now able to come boldly to the throne of God without fear or the sense of guilt and shame.

54

God has made those who hope in Christ for the praise of His glory.

EPHESIANS 1:12

Life is really not about us. It is not about how well we perform, the positions we obtain, or about the things we acquire. For our life here on earth is like a vapor and our glory is like the grass of the field that perishes. Really—it is about Jesus Christ and the power of His Kingdom. That's why we yield all our praise to God and His eternal glory.

55

God will not reject a person of integrity, nor will He lend a hand to the wicked.

JOB 8:20

God will not work with evil nor will He support the proud in their selfish endeavors. In fact He hates pride and resists the proud but gives grace to the humble. He stands behind honest people of character and integrity. God says that the evil man who prospers in his way will soon be cut off, but the meek shall inherit the earth and delight themselves in the abundance of peace.

56

God is our partner walking with us even in death's valley.

PSALM 23:4

God is our faithful partner. He's taken hold of our hand and will never lose His grip on us. He will not abandon us when things get tough and life presents us with many different challenges. He will be there to comfort and guide us through it all. Not even death can stop Him from His faithfulness toward us. He will accompany us even in death—the lowest of all valleys.

57

God can be trusted to keep His promise.

HEBREWS 10:23

Who set the stars perfectly in the sky? Who placed the sun and the moon at their exact locations, providing light and heat to our world? Who raised Christ from the dead and set Him at His own right hand in glory? God did. If He can do all that, we can surely trust Him with the details of our lives and believe that He will keep His promises to us.

58

God's love in us does not insist on its own rights or its own way.

1 CORINTHIANS 13:5

We all struggle with this because we're basically self-centered. It is not easy to quit thinking about ourselves and love with God's love. When we give His love we're not concerned about our own rights or only interested in getting our own way. But God's love in us really cares about the needs of others and actively looks for ways to meet those needs. Find simple ways to express God's love.

59

God has rescued us from the power of darkness and has brought us into the kingdom of his Son, whom he loves.

COLOSSIANS 1:13

Darkness has many negative effects, one of which is ignorance. The Word says that we are destroyed because of a lack of knowledge. You've heard the expression, "When the lights came on." I'll never forget the moment when someone finally told me about Jesus, the light of the world, and how right then and there, He delivered me from darkness and placed me safely in His bright and glorious Kingdom.

60

God has made Jesus, who was crucified, buried, and raised from the dead, both Lord and Christ.

ACTS 2:36

Jesus is the Christ, the Anointed One, and Son of the Living God. He attained His rank and superior position in glory when He gave His life and suffered the horrible death of the crucifixion. It was there that He died for our sins—and it was there He paid for our justification. That is why all praise and honor is due Him—for He is God and Lord of all.

61

God made us His workmanship in Christ and has ordained a plan for our lives.

EPHESIANS 2:10

You are not just some mass-produced object that floated down an industrial assembly line, being stamped out and shaped identically like all the rest. No, you were handmade by God the great master craftsman. You are unique and have been sculpted for a special purpose, created by Christ Himself, designed in Him for good works. Now that's not common. Believe in yourself, you were designed and custom built by God.

62

———∞———

God will set you on high above all nations
of the earth if you will listen to His voice
and do His commands.

DEUTERONOMY 28:1

God has not planned for you to be just an ordinary person. But you are someone very important to Him and responsible to carry out His work in the earth. He created you to be an Ambassador, His Representative sharing the principles of His Kingdom. You're designed to preach the Gospel and make disciples. If you listen to His voice and do His commands He'll set you high above all nations!

63

God is with you wherever you go, so be strong and take courage.

JOSHUA 1:9

Joshua was about to go across the Jordan and take his inheritance, but it was not going to be simply handed to him. There would be enemies and He was going to have to fight for it. You'll have to be strong and fight for your inheritance also—because your enemy does not want you to have it. But fear not, take courage, the Lord is with you wherever you go.

64

God said to Moses, "I AM that I AM." This is what you are to say to the Israelites: "I AM has sent me to you."

EXODUS 3:14

Complete and perfect is the self-existent one—the I AM who dwells in the realm of eternal now. He is without flaw or weakness of any kind. Listen, can you hear Him say, "I AM your strength, I AM your provision, I AM your health, I AM your joy and song, I AM your strong tower and defense against your enemies. I AM your all and all—I AM your God."

65

God commanded you to honor your father and mother so that you will live long and all may go well with you.

DEUTERONOMY 5:16

You may have a real hard time with this commandment because your father or mother doesn't really deserve respect based upon their performance in life. You may have a very legitimate reason to despise or even reject them. But God wants you to honor them. In fact this is the first commandment with a promise that all will go well with you and that you will live long on the earth.

66

God said: "I will certainly bless you, and I will multiply your descendants beyond number.

HEBREWS 6:13

God swore to Abraham that his descendants would multiply greatly. You and I are evidence that His promise was true. That is why our court systems have us lay our right hand on the Holy Bible swearing, "To tell the truth, the whole truth, and nothing but the truth, so help you God." Because there is no higher authority we can swear by than God—even our court system knows that.

67

God purchased our freedom and forgave our sins with the blood of Christ.

COLOSSIANS 1:14

We were all slaves to sin, sold out by Adam to Satan. Mankind had to be purchased back from the authority of evil. Jesus was the only one with the capacity to buy our freedom, but the price was extremely high—it cost Jesus His own blood. He willingly and fearlessly paid the ransom for our sins setting us free from such a dark prison of bondage. Jesus our mighty deliverer!

68

God has a plan for us and works out every-thing in our lives to conform to the purpose of His will.

EPHESIANS 1:11

You may wonder why circumstances happen that don't fit into the plans that you have designed for yourself. Don't worry—these problems are tests, sent to burn out the imperfections in your life. So don't think it's strange when these fiery trials come along and challenge your faith, it is God's way of tempering you like steel—so you'll be strong enough to accomplish the plans He has for your life.

69

---

*God's love is fadeless under all circum-
stances and endures without weakening.*

1 CORINTHIANS 13:7

Human love fails. It's temporary and comes to
an end because it's based upon emotion. God's
love is eternal and endures everything. His love
cannot be weakened by anything or compromised
by any situation. God's love cannot fail. He wants
us to experience this enduring love in our own
lives and give that same unfailing and fadeless
love to others. It must be possible—because He
commanded us to do it.

70

God has reconciled you to Himself by the death of Christ.

COLOSSIANS 1:20

When we reconcile a checking account, we call it "balancing" the checkbook. It means to make an accurate account for every transaction. God is fully aware of every deposit and withdrawal we make and wants our lives to be in balance, fully supplied, and not running in the red. All thanks belong to Christ who paid the debts we could not pay and reconciled us to Himself once and for all.

71

God's grace changes our lives when we understand the truth of the gospel.

COLOSSIANS 1:6

Many people today are attempting to define who God is and what He does. But a man with an *experience with* God is never at the mercy of a man with an *opinion about* God. If you have experienced God's grace yourself and have seen the riches of Christ's mercy in your own life— then another person's *opinion* cannot change what *you* have already *experienced* and *know* to be true about God.

72

God is magnificent; He can never be praised enough. There are no boundaries to His greatness.

PSALM 145:3

There is no limit to God and no way to measure how great and wonderful He really is. All accomplishments of men combined are futile compared to God Almighty. His universe is still expanding ever since He spoke, "Let there be light." We should echo King David who said, "His praise shall continually be in my mouth, and my soul will only boast in the Lord." We cannot praise Him enough.

73

---

*God gives us confidence and hope when we
hear the truth of the good news.*

COLOSSIANS 1:5

Confidence is so important. It can get things
done that nothing else can. Many times in sports
or business it is not necessarily the best team
that wins, but the team with the most confidence. And often that winning spirit and over-
coming attitude comes from great coaching. A
great coach can put into his team the winning
edge. Think about it, we have the greatest coach
ever, the Lord God Almighty.

74

God included us in Christ when we heard the word of truth, the gospel of our salvation.

EPHESIANS 1:13

"The foolishness of preaching" is God's plan to bring salvation to all the earth. His instructions are simple: _Go to the entire world and take the gospel to every person._ If God includes us in Christ after we have heard the word of truth and believed it, then we better get busy _going and taking_ the good news everywhere. We can't expect anyone to believe in something they've never heard about.

75

God has given us redemption through the blood of Christ and the forgiveness of sins.

EPHESIANS 1:7

God has forgiven you and released you from the penalty of your sins. You are free to go. Not only has He forgiven you, but also the Bible says He has separated you from your sins—as far as the east is from the west. He has no record of their existence any longer. All of our sins are blotted out. They are removed and gone forever— now that's good news!

76

God has highly exalted Jesus, and has given Him a name that is above every name.

PHILIPPIANS 2:9

Everything has a name, a title, or an identification of some kind. Some names are highly recognizable and famous. Other names are associated with nobility. But because of Christ's triumphant conquest, God Himself has proclaimed that the name of Jesus is the name above every name. And that is why every knee in heaven and earth shall bow and every tongue will confess throughout all eternity that Jesus Christ is Lord.

77

God is one God, and there is one mediator between God and men, the man Christ Jesus.

1 TIMOTHY 2:5

Some religions and mythologies teach a multiplicity of deities. However, that is simply not true. There is *only* one God and *only* one way to access God and it is *only* through Jesus Christ alone. He is the *only* way to God, and the *only* mediator between God and man. Jesus said, "I am the way the truth and the life and no one can approach the Father except through me."

78

God resists the proud, but gives grace unto the humble.

JAMES 4:6

When someone resists you it means that they won't go along with you. They are not in agreement and they are not moving with you or going in your direction. In the same way God will not support or endorse pride—He's not moving in that direction—He won't go that way—In fact God hates pride and warns us to never become proud. But He gives grace to the humble.

79

God works all things together for good to them that love Him and are called according to His purpose.

ROMANS 8:28

God brings good out of all things for those that are in pursuit of His purposes. You may wonder how He will do it this time, but He always does. Just be patient and keep serving the Lord. Your strength will be renewed and you will rise up with wings like an eagle. Looking at life from that perspective—you will then begin to understand why things happen as they do.

80

God has not given us the spirit of fear, but of power, and of love, and of a sound mind.

2 Timothy 1:7

When my daughter Joy was just a small child she followed the children's minister across the stage in the auditorium who had gone to shut off the lights not realizing that she followed him. From out of the darkness he heard a little voice saying, "God's not given me a spirit of fear, but power, love, and a sound mind." She was quoting God's Word—applying it to her dark circumstances!

81

God is not the author of confusion, but of peace, as in all churches of the saints.

1 CORINTHIANS 14:33

God is not confused about anything and we don't need to be. But confusion can come into our lives through envy and strife. And not only confusion but every evil work. That's bad! The devil is the father of lies and the author of confusion. Stay away from him. God liberally gives us wisdom when we ask and peace that passes understanding when we pray. Let God's peace rule your life.

82

God, who is rich in mercy, made us alive with Christ even when we were dead in transgressions—it is by grace we have been saved.

EPHESIANS 2:5

We don't deserve to be alive with Christ. Our sins and transgressions locked the door cancelling out any approach we may have had to this Holy God. No access. But because He is overflowing with kindness, has an abundance of patience, a wealth of goodness, and a full load of forgiveness, now we can be saved by His grace. We have been given eternal life in Christ Jesus our Lord!

83

God wants your faith to be in His power and not in the wisdom of men.

1 CORINTHIANS 2:5

"Some trust in chariots and some in horses, but we will put our trust in the Lord." The strength of chariot horses is surely great, but God's power is unsurpassable, never ending, and without limit. Even in this age it seems as though mankind has reached a new pinnacle of power through technological advances. We all know anything man-made can fail—but God can never fail. Put your trust in Him.

84

God did not appoint us to suffer wrath but to receive salvation through our Lord Jesus Christ.

1 THESSALONIANS 5:9

Don't let people tell you that God did some mean hateful thing to someone to teach them a lesson or sent sickness to cause someone to grow up spiritually. That's not right or true. All God's wrath was satisfied once and for all through the sacrifice of Jesus at Calvary. Do not be fooled by this dark concept of God. God is light and in Him is no darkness at all.

85

---

*God's power and His wisdom are made
fully known to us in Christ.*

1 CORINTHIANS 1:24

Mankind has power and abilities setting us apart from all of creation because we were created in the image and likeness of God. We are equipped to groom, develop, and even rule over the earth. But mankind on our own without a relationship with Christ will never experience the full power or wisdom available to us. In Him we have unlimited resources at our disposal. You have a business partner—Jesus.

86

---

*God has chosen the weak things of the world
to confound the things that are mighty.*

1 CORINTHIANS 1:27

God does not require the mighty or the strong to carry out His special tasks. Actually He has selected the meek and chosen the lowly to carry out His purposes. He has also chosen to reward the meek and not the mighty—by giving them the earth. You may not have an impressive position or title or even consider yourself as important, but if you are meek—you are very important to God.

87

God promised to live with us and walk among us. He will be our God, and we will be His people.

2 CORINTHIANS 6:16

God wants to live in your house with you. He wants to be a part of your family. He wants to eat, sleep, and work with you every day. He wants to walk with you, talk with you, and help plan your vacations. God likes you and is not ashamed at all to make His home with you. He is planning to stay with you for the rest of your life.

88

God loves and prizes above other things, is unwilling to do without a cheerful, joyous, prompt to do it giver, whose heart is in his giving.

2 CORINTHIANS 9:7

If you want the attention of God then be a giver. If you want to thrill Him—be a cheerful giver! A ready-for-action-giver, whose heart is full of the joy of giving. Someone who is eager and ready to share generously with others. Why? Because God prizes above everything, He is unwilling to do without—a prompt-to-do-it giver. He sets them on top of His list of people to bless.

89

God is merciful and He will not abandon or destroy you or forget the covenant with your forefathers, which He confirmed to them by an oath.

DEUTERONOMY 4:31

It really doesn't matter where you end up, God will be there. He has promised and sworn by His covenant not to leave you or abandon you. He would never destroy you or even hurt you, as some say He will. People will betray you, forsake you, and sometimes leave you far behind. But God will always remain faithful to stay at your side—He has confirmed it with an oath.

90

*God, who provides seed to the sower will
multiply your resources and will increase
the fruits of your righteousness.*

2 CORINTHIANS 9:10

It is God who has made everything, it all
belongs to Him. We are only stewards of what He
provides. If we trust Him, He will increase our
resources, causing us to be plentiful and fully
supplied. When we use our talents to bring forth
good works of righteousness, God is happy. It is
all for His glory and honor and praise that we
increase and bring forth fruit that remains.

91

God is gracious and merciful, and will not turn away His face from you, if ye return unto Him.

2 Chronicles 30:9

You may have said something or done something that really offended a close friend—the conflict was unresolved and they have refused to talk to you. That can really hurt. But here's good news—because of God's gracious mercy and kindness He will not ignore you, refuse to talk to you, He will not abandon you, He won't even turn His face away from you. That's a friend you can trust.

92

---

*God is our refuge and strength and He is a
very present help in times of trouble.*

PSALM 46:1

We are never on our own, never alone, even in
times of trouble God is there. He is always
present and He will help. Sometimes when
people try to help us they just make things
worse. But if we call on the Lord and ask Him
first, then the answers will come and the protec-
tion in our time of trouble will be sure—because
the Lord is in our midst.

93

God is the King of all the earth. Sing to Him a psalm of praise.

PSALM 47:7

Paul and Silas sang praises unto God in the darkness of their prison cell. While they sang out loud at midnight there was a great earthquake and the prison doors were jarred opened. You may be bound up in a prison cell of your own with circumstances looking bleak. I want you to know that God opens doors when we praise Him and sets the captives free when we worship Him.

94

God is our God forever and ever and will be our guide even unto death.

Psalm 48:14

We will never get to the place in life where we no longer need God. We should never try to navigate on our own when He wants to give us His direction every day. Even at the moment of our death He will send His angels to guide us through that final doorway into heaven. He will never loosen His grip on us—for He is our God forever and ever.

95

---

*God has blessed us in the heavenly realms
with all spiritual blessings in Christ.*

EPHESIANS 1:3

God has not withheld any good thing from us,
but has blessed us with all spiritual blessings in
the heavenly realms in Christ. He has accom-
plished this for us by the sacrifice of His only
Son, Jesus, who willingly paid redemption's
price—freeing us from our sins. He has also
liberally given to us His wisdom, understanding,
practical insight, and everything we will ever
need that is essential for our lives.

96

God is our rock and a refuge where no enemy can reach us. Our victory and honor come from Him alone.

PSALM 62:7

One scripture says, "I will set him on high because He has known My Name." I can clearly picture that mountaintop, that incredibly high summit, the fortress that no enemy can climb. Surely we are safe and secure in that high place. The name of Jesus Christ is that rock where we find refuge from each of our adversaries. He alone gives us honor and victory over all of our enemies.

97

God will credit righteousness—for us who believe in Him who raised Jesus our Lord from the dead.

ROMANS 4:24

We have an account in heaven much like our bank accounts here on earth. Whether here or there, we are making deposits and withdrawals. Jesus warned us not to store up treasures here on earth because they eventually lose their value and thieves can break in and steal them—but we are to store our treasures in heaven. We do that by believing in Christ and reflecting His love every day.

98

God has poured out His love into our hearts by the Holy Spirit, whom He has given us.

ROMANS 5:5

Love is tangible. It has substance and form. It is easily distinguished when present and surely noticed when it's missing. It can be felt like the warm sunshine on our face shining from a clear blue sky. It has an amazing power to infuse life, vitalize, and renew. The Holy Spirit was sent to pour God's love into our hearts. Open up and let Him fill your life with His love.

99

God is able to make all grace abound toward you; that ye, always having all sufficiency in all things, may abound to every good work.

Imagine that. All of God's grace is available to you. All sufficiency in all things—so you can abound in every good work. This seems too good to be true. But it is true. God declared this to His people who give generously and cheerfully. This is a promise we need to receive—always having all we need in every area of our lives with nothing missing or anything left out.

100

God through Christ has made you holy and blameless and without a single fault.

COLOSSIANS 1:12

God does not blame you for anything. He does not accuse you or lay your faults at your feet. But through Christ He has made you holy, considers you free from your sins and washed from your transgressions. We can stay in this place of freedom by confessing our faults to one another and by confessing our sins to God—that will keep us clean and in right standing with God.

101

God said, "If we walk in the light as He is in the light we have fellowship one with another and the blood of Jesus cleanses us from all sin."

1 JOHN 1:7

There is nothing in this world that can take the place of honesty. In fact Thomas Jefferson said that, "Honesty is the first chapter in the book of wisdom." We all know how it feels to be lied to—it demeans us and destroys our confidence in others. Walking in fellowship means we are open with people, genuine and true, without a hidden motive. So remember, always walk in the light.

The End

P.S. For more Bible teaching and a chance to share in an online Christian community join us at: www.wordandspiritbooks.com

Author Bio

Chuck Coggins is the president and director of international development for a humanitarian organization called HELPS. The main thrust of HELPS is *bringing together people and resources from around the world*. The organization is focusing primarily in the areas of Health, Education, Leadership, and Planning Services. Chuck and his wife Connie have participated in numerous business and ministry seminars in Mexico, Botswana, Kenya, Zimbabwe, India, Peru, Jamaica, and Romania.

Chuck and Connie have been happily married for thirty-three years have seven children and four grandsons. They are also the founders and leaders of the Carpenter's Workshop Community of Asbury United Methodist Church in Tulsa, Oklahoma.